A Wintry Tale

By

Iris Dingle and Martin Flatters.

Copyright © Iris Dingle, 2018 Published: December 2018 by FCM Publishing

www.fcmpublishing.co.uk

ISBN: 978-1-9164398-8-7

Paperback Edition

All rights reserved.

The right of Iris Dingle & Martin Flatters to be identified as the authors of this Work has been asserted by them in accordance with sections 77 and 78 of the Copyright, Designs and Patents Act 1988.

No part of this publication may be reproduced, stored in retrieval system, copied in any form or by any means, electronic, mechanical, photocopying, recording or otherwise transmitted without written permission from the publisher. You must not circulate this book in any format.

Copyright of all illustrations and imagery used within remains solely with their originator. All Illustrations by Iris Dingle

This book is dedicated to our newly arrived granddaughter,

The Princess of Fairies, Isobel.

Christmas 2016.

At the coldest part of winter, when the snow is falling and the ice is forming.

Isobel the Fairy Princess longs for the sun, of a sun that seems far away.

Come back...come back...come back.

The winters snow lay deep, and the polar bears were fast asleep.

Suddenly, the polar bears woke.

What could it be? What could it be? What could it be?

In the frozen south, the baby penguin sits on his mother's feet, keeping him snug and warm.

She tells her chick that they will soon be coming...

"Who's coming?" asks the little chick.

"Shhhhh" the mother says,

"We have to wait...we have to wait...we have to wait."

The lonely reindeer walks through the frozen forest.

Mile after mile without any rest.

With no house or home, his winter coat keeps him warm.

From winter's harshest storm.

What is he looking for...looking for...looking for?

Whooooosh... The owl flies silently through the forest.

"Hoot hoot!"

She has a message for the animals.

"Not long now dears" she hoots to delighted ears.

"Not long...not long...not long!"

On the coast there is a mighty storm, the waves high and cold.

The wind so strong the puffin has to walk, not fly.

The puffin sits and mutters,

"Come soon...come soon...come soon."

In the garden, a little blue tit sits on the snow covered branch.

The owl told the little bird he must be ready.

"It's coming soon."

"What, what, what?", says the little bird.

The snow silently falls. The dog comes out of the warm house and into the garden, he sniffs!

"There is something in the air.

There is a different feel, it feels like a change is coming."

A change is coming...a change is coming...soon.

The snow continues to fall in the garden, the fluffy cat, swishes her tail.

"Meow, meow!"

She thinks she sees something in the distance! "What can it be?!" she excitedly asks.

She sits and waits for it to come closer...come closer...come closer.

The little red squirrel sits on the snow, his nose is twitching.

"My nuts are cold and this winter's getting rather old", he says.

Come soon...come soon...come soon.

The fox and the hare meet in the snow covered fields.

He asks the hare, "what have you heard?"

"It's coming...it's coming...it's coming!"

Brock the badger is awoken from his warm winter's set.

"Who has woken me?"

Something's coming...something's coming...something's coming!

Flying through the cold winter's air, everything is frozen everywhere.

Even the lakes are frozen too, so the swans fly on.

For they know it would soon to be coming.

"We must fly on...fly on...fly on!"

The goat shivers in the snow.

"Baa baa it's cold...it's cold, baa baa!

It is coming soon...coming soon...coming soon!

The donkey who guards the farm and watches.

"Heehaw! Heehaw! Heehaw!" he calls.

"I can see it coming. It will soon be here, soon be here, we must be ready!

Heehaw! Heehaw! Heehaw!"

On a starry midwinter night, the animals meet up and walk into the forest, looking, searching!

In the middle of the forest, they are drawn to a bright, shiny, sparkling tree covered in stars and mirrors. They all gathered around the tree.

The wise owl tells them of a time before when people used to welcome the return of the sun after the long winter months, by tying mirrors and gifts to the tree.

Men may have forgotten but the animals still remember.

On midwinter's day, as the sun rises on the farm, the dogs await the coming of the winter visitor, who brings gifts, health and good fortune to the family, one and all.

About the Authors

Martin & Iris retired in 2013 to make a new life in Central Portugal, they live on an olive farm high in the beautiful mountains with their animals, which include a donkey, a small herd of goats and several dogs.

Iris & Martin were so enchanted by the individual characters of their animals that they were inspired to write a unique Christmas story for their grandchildren to enjoy.

Iris is a well-known and loved artist, while Martin looks after the farm.

Featuring:

Mr Xister, The Donkey

Esther, The Goat

Gaia, Sky and Bruyn; The Dogs

www.ingramcontent.com/pod-product-compliance
Lightning Source LLC
Chambersburg PA
CBHW042248100526
44587CB00002B/70